Keeping Unusual Pets

SALAMANDERS

Peter Heathcote

Heinemann
LIBRARY

www.heinemann.co.uk/library

To order:
☎ Phone 44 (0) 1865 888066
🗎 Send a fax to 44 (0) 1865 314091
💻 Visit the Heinemann bookshop at www.heinemann.co.uk/library to browse our catalogue and order online.

First published in Great Britain by Heinemann Library, Halley Court, Jordan Hill, Oxford OX2 8EJ, part of Harcourt Education.
Heinemann is a registered trademark of Harcourt Education Ltd.

Editorial: Nancy Dickmann, Louise Galpine and Tanvi Rai
Design: Ron Kamen and Celia Floyd
Picture Research: Rebecca Sodergren
Production: Séverine Ribierre

Originated by Dot Gradations
Printed in China by WKT Company Limited

ISBN 0 431 12417 5
08 07 06 05 04
10 9 8 7 6 5 4 3 2 1

British Library Cataloguing in Publication Data

Heathcote, Peter
  Salamanders. – (Keeping unusual pets)
  1. Salamanders as pets – Juvenile literature
  I. Title
  639.3'785

A full catalogue record for this book is available from the British Library.

Acknowledgements

The publishers would like to thank the following for permission to reproduce photographs:

Ardea/Mary Clay: p. 5 (top); CORBIS/Joe McDonald: p. 31; CORBIS/Peter Johnson: p. 22 (bottom); FLPA: pp. 8 (top), 42; FLPA/B Borrell: p. 21 (bottom); FLPA/Chris Mattison: p. 7 (top); FLPA/Francoise Merlet: pp. 5 (bottom), 9; FLPA/Yossi Eshbol: p. 7 (bottom); Maria Joannou: p. 43 (top); NHPA/Daniel Heuclin: pp. 6, 8 (bottom), 20; NHPA/Stephen Dalton: p. 4; NPL/Martin Gabriel: p. 30 (bottom); SPL/K H Kjeldsen: p. 40; SPL/Sinclair Stammers: p. 39 (bottom); Trevor Clifford: p. 30 (top); Tudor Photography: pp. 10, 11 (top), 11 (bottom), 12, 13 (top), 13 (bottom), 14, 15 (top), 15 (bottom), 16, 17 (top), 17 (bottom), 18 (top), 18 (bottom), 19, 21 (top), 22 (top), 23 (top), 23 (bottom), 24, 25, 26, 27 (top), 27 (bottom), 28, 29 (top), 29 (bottom), 32, 33, 34, 35 (top), 35 (bottom), 36, 37, 38, 39 (top), 41 (top), 41 (bottom), 43 (bottom), 44 (left), 44 right), 45.

Cover photograph of the salamander reproduced with permission of Corbis/Lynda Richardson.

The publishers would like to thank Yarnton Nurseries for their assistance in the preparation of this book.

Every effort has been made to contact copyright holders of any material reproduced in this book. Any omissions will be rectified in subsequent printings if notice is given to the publishers.

Disclaimer

Contents

What is a salamander? 4

Salamander facts 6

Is a salamander for you? 8

Choosing a salamander 10

What do I need? 12

Caring for your salamander 20

Can we make friends? 26

Fun time together 30

Keeping my salamander healthy 34

Some health problems 38

When a salamander dies 42

Keeping records 44

Glossary 46

Useful addresses 47

More books to read 47

Helpful websites 47

Index 48

Any words appearing in the text in bold, **like this**, are explained in the Glossary.

What is a salamander?

Salamanders are **amphibians**. There are over 300 kinds of salamander, and they are easily identifiable. They have short bodies, a long tail, four legs and a well-developed head. Most salamanders available in pet stores have been captured from the wild. There is little difference between a 'wild' and 'tame' salamander's behaviour.

An axolotl is an aquatic amphibian. This means that it can only breathe under water and not in air.

Many people confuse salamanders with lizards, but they are not even related. Lizards are **reptiles** and have a very different lifecycle. Young salamanders **metamorphose** from **larvae** into adults, whereas reptiles hatch as mini-adults and then grow without metamorphosis. Unlike reptiles with their tough, protective skin that allows nothing in or out, salamanders both absorb and lose water through their skin and can **dehydrate** very quickly. They must keep their **porous** skin moist, remaining in damp places to absorb water. This means they do not have to drink from a water bowl!

The salamander's skin contains many **glands** carrying out different jobs. Some keep the skin moist, others release poison. Salamanders are poisonous to eat and so are protected against **predators**.

4

In the wild, salamanders eat various insects, as well as molluscs and the occasional frog or small mouse. It is essential to reproduce this diet in captivity if your salamanders are to stay healthy. Salamanders also shed their skin and eat it once it has come off. But if the weather is too cold, your salamander will stop shedding altogether until the temperature increases. All amphibians are cold-blooded – they rely on their surroundings to keep their bodies warm enough to survive.

An earthworm makes a tasty treat for a hungry salamander.

Your responsibilities:

- Never buy a pet without first considering the good and the bad points.
- Check with your local authorities to see whether a license to keep salamanders is necessary.
- Young children are not allowed to buy pets, so have an adult take you to the pet store.
- Never buy a pet because you feel sorry for it in the pet store.
- Taking animals from the wild harms their species' future survival. Wherever possible, purchase **captive-bred** salamanders.
- Join your local **herpetological** society to keep up to date with the latest salamander care information.

These wild salamanders are hiding in a burrow.

Salamander facts

Two common **species** of salamander kept as pets are the tiger salamander (*Ambystoma tigrinum*) and the fire salamander (*Salamandra salamandra*). The tiger salamander lives in North America and can reach a length of more than 20 centimetres. Outside of the **breeding season** it will spend a great deal of time hiding in burrows that have been dug out by small mammals, and so has earned the nickname 'the mole salamander'. The fire salamander is found throughout Europe, South-west Asia and some parts of North-west Africa. As with the tiger salamander, the fire salamander can reach an adult size of more than 20 centimetres.

These two salamander species are both terrestrial (live on land) but an important difference between the two is that the tiger prefers to spend its time alone, whereas the fire enjoys the company of other salamanders of the same species. However, the fire may be less willing to come out to see you, and it is the tiger who may be bold enough to feed from its owner's tweezers.

Top tip

The weight of salamanders varies tremendously; remember to record the weight of your pet every week. It is important that it is not losing weight as this could indicate a medical problem.

Some salamanders like to live in a group. In the wild they often stick together instead of living alone.

Tiger salamanders are found in the central valley of California and in the low foothills by the coast.

Day or night?

One downside of keeping salamanders as pets is that they are naturally **nocturnal**. To overcome this, close the curtains in the room where it is housed and wait for a while. Then turn on a lamp with a dark-coloured bulb inside it, and you should be able to watch its activities without disturbing it too much. It is important that you do not confuse its waking and sleeping times and so it is better to close the curtains an hour before you go to bed, allowing you some time to watch it in the tank.

Fire salamanders live in damp forests in hilly regions.

Lifelong friends

Fire salamanders can live for over 14 years. This means that you may well be friends throughout many changes in your own life, including going to college or leaving home.

7

Is a salamander for you?

Deciding whether or not a salamander is the right pet for you can be very hard. If you are the wrong sort of person to keep a salamander then you and your pet could be unhappy for as long as its 14-year lifespan. Remember to take your time when deciding whether this is going to be a long-term friend for you. As with all pets, there are good and not-so-good points about keeping creatures in captivity.

Salamander good points:

- They can live for a long time.
- They can be purchased as babies and you can watch them grow.
- They only need feeding once every two or three days.
- They only need to be cleaned once a week (although spot cleaning should be done daily).
- They do not make any noise to disturb the neighbours.
- Missing one day of food will have no effect on your salamander.

If you get a juvenile amphibian you can watch it change as it grows!

Keeping a salamander means you will have to handle live worms and other creepy crawlies!

Salamander not-so-good points:

- Salamanders carry diseases that can be passed onto humans unless routine hygiene precautions are taken.
- Fire salamanders may well live for over 14 years, whilst tiger salamanders can reach an age of 25 years. Is this too long a commitment for you to make?
- The salts and oils in your skin can damage a salamander's skin and so handling your pet is not a good idea unless absolutely necessary.
- Their skin dries out very quickly so they cannot be taken out for walks.
- It can be very expensive to set up properly the salamander's **terrarium.**
- Veterinary treatment can be expensive and finding a veterinarian experienced in **amphibians** can prove difficult. This may mean that if your pet is sick you have to travel in order to find someone who can help.
- You will need to keep live insects as feed in your home and there is always a chance some may escape!

A salamander's skin is moist and sticky. Many terrestrial salamanders don't have lungs; they breathe through their skin!

Choosing a salamander

It is difficult to select your new long-term friend from only a brief meeting at your local pet store. You should have many questions and, before you commit to purchasing your new companion, take a good look around the store.

Remember to check the salamander for signs of ill health before you buy it.

Things you should see:

- Insects on sale should be in good condition; poor food means poor pets!
- Cages should be clean and well-ventilated (airy), with fresh water. Remember salamanders absorb everything through their skin; if they are living in dirty water they will be unhealthy.
- The staff should be helpful and offer plenty of advice.
- Specimens should be **captive-bred** where possible, with feeding records available.

Things to avoid:

- Dirty water bowls
- Dirty cages
- **Wild-caught** specimens.

One or two salamanders?

It is better to keep tiger salamanders alone, as they are very territorial and will often fight to the death. If you want to keep more than one, then keep two females in a large **terrarium**. Males are more likely to start cage fights. Fire salamanders, however, are happier kept in a group (this is quite unusual for salamanders, outside of the **breeding season**). But still give your **colony** of fire salamanders a large cage otherwise fights will occur!

At the pet store you may see a terrarium with several fire salamanders kept together.

Male or female?

If, at any time in the future, you are thinking of keeping more than one salamander, then start off with a female. If you keep a **species** that lives happily in a group, then it is easier to begin with a female. This is because the introduction of another salamander of either sex to a female is less likely to cause a problem than if you introduced a male to a male. A simple mistake could lead to a deadly fight.

The salamander cage should be clean with fresh water. It should look interesting with places for the salamanders to hide.

Buying your salamander

The best place to buy your salamander is from a private breeder. If you have problems finding someone in your neighbourhood, why not join your local **herpetological** society? Remember that if you cannot find a salamander that has been captive-bred, you should try to find one that has adapted well to captivity.

11

What do I need?

It is very important to keep your salamander inside a special cage called a **terrarium**. This allows you to control the **humidity** of the salamander's environment as well as making sure that crickets and other live food cannot escape into your home. It is also important not to let your salamander run unsupervised around your home; **amphibians** carry diseases that humans can catch. Also, your salamander may become injured whilst taking a closer look at the family cat or dog.

A terrarium is also called a vivarium. It is important to set up your terrarium before you bring your salamander home.

Materials

You can buy a terrarium from a pet shop or make your own. It should be made mainly of glass as the inside will become very damp. To prevent **parasites** entering the cage and water leaking from it, all internal joints should be sealed with a silicon rubber sealant. A wooden or polystyrene construction built around the outside of the glass tank and covering both ends, the back and base, will help the cage **maintain** a stable temperature. A dark wood will help to reduce stress for your **nocturnal** salamander, and perhaps encourage him to come out before you go to bed.

Be careful to ensure that all the edges of the terrarium are sealed with silicon.

Shape and size

Ground-dwelling salamanders prefer a longer, rather than taller, terrarium. This allows them to investigate and behave freely. In the wild, fire salamanders are slow to explore and move around; a terrarium measuring 60 centimetres long, 30 centimetres high and 30 centimetres wide should comfortably house two or three. Tiger salamanders enjoy exploring, and benefit from longer enclosures measuring about 90 centimetres long.

Good ventilation is essential. This cage has fine mesh ventilation holes built into it.

Ventilation

All amphibians require air in order to survive. Ventilation (making the terrarium airy) can be achieved by purchasing a terrarium lid with a panel of fine mesh holes built into it. You can also add vents at the sides. Vents should not be placed at the same height on opposite sides of the cage as this can create a **draught**, and cause sickness. Instead, place them at significantly different heights.

Heating

There should be no need to heat the terrarium for salamanders living in your home. The fire salamander needs temperatures between 13–19 °C and the tiger salamander between 15–21 °C. Temperatures for both salamander **species** must not increase above 21 °C as this may cause death.

Keeping cool

Think carefully before you position your terrarium. Is there an unheated room that stays cool throughout the year? Air-conditioning can assist in keeping salamanders cool, but it is important to replace moisture in the air and maintain sufficient humidity levels. Alternatively, fans can be used on a low setting, pointing away from the cage so that the salamander feels no draughts.

Be very careful about setting the right temperature in the room where you place the terrarium, as it can affect your pet's health.

Humidity

Amphibian skin dries very quickly, causing a range of health problems. Keep the environment humid at all times. Ventilation will alter the humidity level (an increase in ventilation will decrease humidity and vice versa) so use a humidity meter to keep levels around 70 per cent.

Shedding

Sometimes your salamander will need extra humidity. When your salamander starts to shed its skin, spray it with a gentle mist of warm water to assist the process (allow the water to stand overnight so that any chlorine in it can evaporate). Once it has shed, make sure that no pieces of skin are left on its toes or around its tail as these can restrict blood-flow and cause it to lose its limbs.

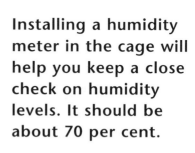

Spraying your salamander can help it in shedding its skin.

What can happen if the humidity is wrong?

- **Respiratory** problems
- Blisters and skin infections
- Eye infections
- **Infestation** problems
- Possible death.

Installing a humidity meter in the cage will help you keep a close check on humidity levels. It should be about 70 per cent.

15

Ultraviolet light

Some **ultraviolet light** is important for your salamander to have healthy skin and vision. It is generally not essential to use UV lights with salamanders, but opinion on this matter is constantly changing. Check on the latest ideas with your **herpetological** society.

Ultraviolet light should be installed in the cage if possible. We manage to get our ultraviolet light from sunshine but your pet needs some extra help getting it.

Substrate

Substrate is placed at the bottom of the terrarium to absorb waste products. You can use leaf litter and **sphagnum moss** for this. You will need to remove soiled substrate from the cage and change it completely on a regular basis. Ideally, the entire contents of the terrarium should be changed and replaced with fresh substrate and cleaned furniture once a week to prevent bacterial and fungal growth.

Any substrate you use must be clean and chemical-free. Why not use a mixture of soil and leaf litter with one area covered in moss? You can collect leaf litter from the garden if no pesticides have been used, or buy protected moss from a pet store or other retail outlet.

The subtrate should have about 9 cm of soil covered by 2 cm of leaf litter.

Bury a water bowl in your substrate so that it is level with the rim of the bowl, allowing easy access to your salamander. It will be happiest if it has around 9 centimetres of soil covered with 2 centimetres of leaf litter and a water bowl large enough to sit in.

Your salamander should start exploring its cage more often once it gets used to its new home.

Cage furniture

This makes the enclosure look pleasing to the eye and provides **hides**. Hides are areas that allow your pet salamander to feel safe and secure from **predators**. These can be easily made from a cardboard box, or plant pot with a hole cut in the side or lid. Hides should be placed throughout the enclosure to allow the salamander to explore the cage while feeling safe. It is your responsibility to help your new pet live a happy, stimulated life with you.

You can make lots of interesting furniture for your pet using your creative talents!

Plants

Real plants are an attractive addition to the cage, but check that they are not poisonous. Plastic plants often break into smaller pieces and can be swallowed, easily causing a bowel blockage. Contact your local herpetological group for an up-to-date list of 'safe' living plants.

Adding plants to the cage makes it look more attractive and gives your pet more places to explore. But always make sure they are safe to have near your salamanders.

Hygiene

Once you have brought your salamander home, the terrarium should be cleaned regularly with a mild disinfectant or marketed cleaner. Most household cleaners are safe to use but avoid bleach and strong, heavy-duty cleaners. Rinse the cage with clean water in order to prevent any chemicals being absorbed by the salamander's skin. Pay particular attention to corners. Dry well before replacing the amphibian.

To keep your salamander healthy you should rinse out and refill its water dish every day.

Top tips

- General hygiene is important after handling animals and also after cleaning the terrarium.
- Wash your hands with a mild disinfectant or **antibacterial** soap.
- Food and water bowls should be removed, cleaned and replaced daily. Use either bottled water or tap water that has been left to stand for several hours to allow any chlorine in it to evaporate.
- Be careful not to place your pet's food and water containers on kitchen surfaces as this may spread disease.

Caring for your salamander

Salamanders are very hard to breed in captivity. This often means that the animal you have chosen was born in the wild and has been used to travelling freely and selecting many different foods. Salamanders often have their own favourite foods, and may not be keen on your choices! Several different commercially available foods are suitable to feed to your salamander. At different stages in your pet's life you will need to change the food being offered.

Baby salamanders (**larvae**) live in water and will feed on different foods to those of adults. It can be surprising to realize that your salamander is **carnivorous** from the time it hatches! The live food it eats will include **daphnia**, mealworms, crickets, waxworms, small locusts and garden insects, as well as brine shrimps.

Salamander larvae have gills just like fish do. They can only breathe under water.

Top tips

- Keep your waxworms in a cool place to keep them alive before feeding them to your salamander.
- Small mice can be offered as an occasional treat, though these are quite fatty and so should only be offered rarely. Mice are available ready-frozen from pet stores and should be thawed out overnight in a cool room before being offered to your pet.

What to feed?

To prevent illness make sure that the food you feed to your salamander has been 'gut loaded'. This means that the insects are placed in a secure container with good quality fruit and vegetation for at least 24 hours before being fed to your pet.

This larva is ready to metamorphose.

Feed the food! The crickets and mealworms and others should get a feast of fresh food before your pet feasts on them.

Larvae to metamorphosis

By the time tiger salamanders change into their adult form and lose their **gills**, they will be fully grown. As larvae they are constantly hungry and want to grow as quickly as possible to give themselves the best chance of survival in the outside world. Tiger larvae will start to feed on daphnia and then brine shrimps which can be bought at your local garden centre or aquarium supplies shop. Special kits are available to let you hatch and rear brine shrimps at home; this is fun to do and lets you know exactly what you are feeding your pet. As the salamander grows, larger food can be offered. Try offering earthworms and medium-sized crickets.

Metamorphosed adults

An adult salamander living on land and breathing air has a wide choice of foods. Earthworms and crickets are still favourites, but you can now try larger crickets as well as moths and grasshoppers. It is quite acceptable to place small numbers of crickets and other food items inside the enclosure and watch that they are eaten quickly. But do not leave uneaten insects in the cage for long periods. Offer your salamander food every day and feed it as much as it wishes to consume. Use a variety of food items at each feed; just like us, salamanders prefer variety in their diet.

Always use tweezers when offering food to your salamander to avoid accidental bites!

Top tip

Many salamander-keepers use floating food sticks that are designed for other animals. These may not be harmful, but until research proves this, use foods that are known to cause no long-term harm to your pet.

Brine shrimps make an ideal lunch for a salamander.

Vitamin and mineral supplements

In the wild, salamanders eat other animals that have spent their day eating fruit and vegetables. In captivity, salamanders eat live food that has been artificially reared and may have had no extra nourishment for days. This means they may not be getting all the nutrients they need.

There is much confusion over mineral supplements and how to use them. Most supplements come in powder form. A general multivitamin can be used weekly and should also be placed on the insects. Do not put anything in the water other than a good quality water-purifier.

Place the required amount of supplement in a bag, add the insects and shake until the food is coated in powder.

Treats

Waxworms are an acceptable treat for salamanders, but remember that too many are unhealthy as they have a high fat content! Cat food or dog food can cause liver and kidney damage to salamanders and can prove fatal. An occasional spoonful will have no long-lasting effects, but don't make this a regular food.

It can be quite interesting to observe how your pet catches the live food that you put in the cage.

Top tip
Do not leave the water bowl in the cage when you are offering supplement-coated insects, as the insects could drown in the bowl or wash off the supplement powder.

Nail care

Salamanders use their feet and nails for burrowing into hidden areas such as moss. Check that your pet's feet are clean and free from any sign of injury or disease. If you are in doubt, ask your veterinarian.

Holiday care

Try not to leave your pet alone when you go on holiday, even for just a weekend. Ask a responsible person to take care of your salamander while you are away. Many pet stores and **herpetological** societies can suggest someone who is experienced in caring for **amphibians**.

When you go on holiday, you should leave a list of care instructions for the person looking after your salamander.

Transporting your salamander

It is best not to transport your salamander, especially on long journeys, but if you must move it, for example to take it to the veterinarian, then it is safest to place your salamander in a container that is only slightly larger than it. Make sure it is well-ventilated and that the box is strong and clearly marked with the words 'This way up'. Keep the box out of direct sunshine and **draughts** and never leave it unattended.

Salamanders can die in hot motor vehicles, so plan your journey well and keep your pet with you at all times. Remember that it will need to be kept moist on the journey, so soak a clean cloth in warm water that is safe for its use, then wring the cloth out until it is damp and use it to line the box.

The box you use to transport your salamander should be well-ventilated and only slightly bigger then your pet.

Checking your salamander

It is very important that you check your pet regularly to make sure it is well. Check that:

- your salamander has no worms in its faeces
- there is no fungus growing on its skin
- your salamander has no unusual lumps or swellings, particularly around its mouth
- no skin is stuck around its toes or tail
- its eyes are clear and bright and that its nose is not blocked.

If you notice any of these problems, consult a veterinarian immediately.

25

Can we make friends?

Salamanders taken from the wild will not be used to people or cages. When you bring your new salamander home, you may want to show it to your friends right away, but remember to look at things from its point of view. It will be frightened on arrival at its new home and will want to hide away from the world in a safe hole.

Be gentle and take your time!

Do not be tempted to look underneath the log or poke your salamander! Your patience will pay off when after a few days it will start to explore its new **terrarium**. The hardest thing is remembering that you should not handle it at all (except in an emergency or for cage cleaning). This is for its own good and something that you should think a lot about before choosing a salamander as a pet.

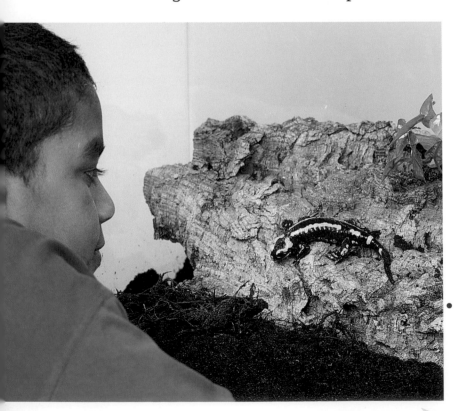

Watching your salamander explore the terrarium that you set up can be very satisfying.

Picking up your salamander

Once you arrive home you will need to place your salamander into its cage. Wash your hands with clean water but no soap or detergents. Make sure that your hands are still very damp, as this will stop your new pet sticking to you and reduce the risk of damaging its skin. Scoop it up underneath its stomach and place it quickly into the terrarium. It is tempting to walk around the house showing your friends and family how beautiful it is, but this will create stress and possible injury for your salamander.

Always wet your hands before you handle your salamander.

Remember to wash your hands with soap after you touch your pet.

27

Top tip

You should weigh your new pet on a set of kitchen scales as soon as you arrive home. Make a note of how much your salamander weighs. This information can be used to make a chart that will help you to track your salamander's development as it grows up with you.

Use a separate container to the one used to weigh foods that you will eat. Keep your salamander's own special 'tub' for this use in the future.

Meeting other salamanders

It is not a good idea to introduce your salamander to others unless it is a fire salamander or it is the **breeding season**, which extends from mid-January to early April. Tiger salamanders are solitary animals, so it is better not to risk injury just for the sake of having more than one!

Never let your pet meet other animals such as dogs and cats. While they may not intend to hurt it, they may think it is a toy. Every year many **amphibians** are killed by the family dog or cat. Remember to make sure that the lid of your enclosure is very securely fastened, so other pets cannot open up the terrarium and reach the salamander inside.

28

Be careful!

Even when tiger salamanders meet during their breeding season, some still suffer injury or death. Fire salamanders should be of a similar size when they are introduced and two males should never be placed together.

Always lock the terrarium door! Any other pets you may have can get quite curious about the new arrival.

Biting

It is unusual to be bitten by a salamander, mainly because they are not handled very often! It is not common for them to be aggressive towards humans, but remember that your hands are very hot compared to the low temperature of a salamander's skin.

If a salamander bites you it is best simply to wait, and then after a few seconds it will let go as your hands become too warm for comfort! Don't try to pull it off you as this will cause more damage to you and may well injure your pet.

If you get bitten remember to wash with clean water straight away, and ask an adult to help you disinfect the injury.

29

Fun time together

Before you start to have fun with your salamander, it is important to think about what it might consider to be fun. Different animals have different ideas of fun. Dogs and cats may enjoy playing games with you, and even rabbits and birds can form lasting bonds of affection with their owners. However, salamanders are different.

In many cases an animal's idea of fun depends on how it lives in the wild. For example, dogs are naturally playful and tend to live in packs in the wild. A pet dog will form a strong bond with its owners because it sees them as part of its pack. Salamanders kept as pets will be most comfortable in conditions similar to what they are used to in the wild, and they will show most of the same behaviours.

Dogs love human contact – salamanders behave very differently.

Try to provide your pet salamander with conditions that are as close to its natural habitat as possible.

30

Behaviour in the wild

Fire salamanders are very shy and spend a great deal of their time hiding from other animals, especially **predators**, under rocks and logs. Their natural habitat consists of well-shaded woodland with ponds and slow-moving streams, and they will stay in the same general area for many years. The tiger salamander will spend much of its time burrowing in soil, which is not very surprising if you remember that it belongs to a group nicknamed 'mole salamanders'. A pet salamander will continue to display these **solitary** behaviours.

If you want a pet that you can spend hours actively playing with and taking for walks outside, then a salamander is not for you. The emotional bond of friendship that exists between humans and their pet dogs and cats cannot be built up in the same way with an **amphibian**.

Salamanders in the wild have to be careful about exposing themselves to predators. In fact, sometimes larger salamanders eat smaller salamanders!

How can I make my salamander happy?

It is likely that a salamander's sense of happiness comes from feeling safe and secure where it is living. It is very important to give your salamander a good quality cage and to change the layout of its environment every few weeks. This variety encourages it to explore its cage and gives it something to do, keeping it alert and active.

Top tips

- Keep a selection of **hides** and rocks of different shapes and sizes.
- Once every so often, after cleaning the **terrarium**, change the position of the rocks.
- Make sure that there is always a hide in the middle of the enclosure to prevent any feelings of insecurity. With a central hide it is easy for the salamander to hide away from any point in the cage.
- Halves of ceramic flowerpots are excellent hides; if you can't get hold of one, why not bury half of the pot in the cage **substrate**?

If there isn't a hide in the middle of the cage, you can rearrange the furniture to make one.

Does my salamander mind not being handled?

If you have ever had a pet dog or cat, you will know that they love attention and want you to spend lots of time petting them. Salamanders do not have the same needs. In the wild, other animals do not handle salamanders and so it is not necessary as part of their daily needs or to make them feel happy and well. They may actually feel threatened by handling. Although it might seem cruel to leave your salamander alone in its cage, it will not be lonely – in fact it will probably be happier that way.

As the proud owner of a beautiful salamander, it can be very difficult to resist the temptation to pick it up and take it round to show all of your friends. But as a responsible pet owner it is your job to remember that this sort of treatment will cause your pet serious distress. Too much **stress** can even kill a salamander. It is very, very important to think carefully about what it is you want to achieve by keeping a salamander. If you want to be able to handle your pet in order to build up a relationship with it, then a salamander is not for you!

While you leave your salamander on its own to explore its cage and relax, you can find out more about how they live in the wild.

Keeping my salamander healthy

Before buying your salamander, telephone a few veterinarians in your neighbourhood and ask whether or not they are happy to deal with your type of pet. All veterinarians are qualified to deal with **amphibians**, but some prefer to refer you to a colleague with a special interest in this area. Consultations and treatment can be expensive and might involve travelling some distance, depending on where you live. When you visit your veterinarian, take your record-book and charts along with you. Even if they haven't seen many salamanders, your veterinarian may well wish to research them so that they are better able to help you with any future problems that may occur.

Top tip

There is no need to ask the vet to **neuter** your salamander. It is a procedure that is rarely carried out. Breeding is prevented by the pet owner by choosing only one sex of salamander to keep.

There are no special **vaccinations** needed either for you or your amphibian. It is, however, advisable to let your doctor know that you are keeping salamanders and make sure that your own **tetanus** vaccine is up to date.

If your salamander gets sick, you should take it to see a veterinarian as soon as possible.

Can I prevent common diseases?

Most of the time a visit to the veterinarian with a salamander is due to the owner's poor care and cage **maintenance**. Over 90 per cent of exotic pet diseases do not occur in the wild. This shows you how important it is to take proper care of your salamander.

Make sure that the temperature in the cage is correct and that it doesn't get too warm. Try to keep your salamander in conditions as similar as possible to those in which it would have lived in the wild. It is important to have your salamander wormed every six months to make sure that they don't have any internal **parasites** that could lead to death.

This wild salamander looks alert and perfectly healthy. Make sure you check on your pet's behaviour every day so that illnesses don't go unnoticed.

A veterinarian can worm your salamander orally.

Zoonoses

You will also need to keep yourself healthy whilst caring for your salamander. Zoonoses are diseases which may be picked up from animals. The best-known amphibian zoonosis is infection by the bacteria *Salmonella*. Many different types of *Salmonella* have been found in amphibians, several of which have been found to cause disease in humans. The very young, very old and people who are unwell are most at risk of picking up an infection from amphibians. This can easily be avoided if you follow these simple rules:

- Wash your hands, preferably with an **antibacterial** handwash, after handling any amphibian, cage or accessory.
- Wear gloves whilst cleaning enclosures.
- Disinfect cages regularly.
- Keep very young children away from amphibians. Older children should be supervised when cleaning amphibians.
- Keep amphibians and their equipment away from food preparation areas.

Cleaning the terrarium regularly will help keep both you and your salamander healthy.

A clean salamander is a healthy one

The most important way to make sure your salamander stays healthy is to keep its **terrarium** nice and clean. When you clean it you will have to move your salamander to a temporary home.

Find a small container with a secure lid and then make some holes in the top, making sure that the smooth side of the hole edge is on the inside, so the salamander cannot hurt itself or damage its skin. Place a small amount of **sphagnum moss** inside the container and then wet your hands just before you lift your salamander into its temporary housing. Make sure that the lid is securely fastened and that it is placed away from household dangers, such as the possibility of being stepped on by another member of your family.

It only takes a few minutes to prepare a safe holding place for your pet but it can mean the difference between life and death!

Top tip

Remember that the requirements for being happy and healthy apply to the container you place it in for cleaning, as much as they do at any other time.

Once you are happy that your salamander is secure and away from danger, you are free to clean the cage at your leisure. When the enclosure has been cleaned, place the salamander back into its home and clean the holding container, ready for the next time.

Some health problems

Poor diet or unsuitable environmental conditions cause most diseases commonly seen in captive **amphibians**. Many of the problems we see in pet salamanders are simply not found in wild ones. The more a salamander feels at home in a well-thought out cage, the healthier your animal will be, saving you a great deal of **stress** and expensive veterinary bills.

Top tip

Any medication that is used to make your salamander feel better can also, in some rare cases, make it feel unwell. No prescribed treatment is ever completely safe, and so the advantages must outweigh the disadvantages when deciding with the veterinarian what to do for the best.

Fungal Infections

If you see a fuzzy white speck or lump on your salamander's skin, this may mean that it has a fungal infection. This **fungus** lives on the outside of the salamander's skin and is called *Saprolegnia*. Suggested treatment for these kinds of fungi is as follows:

- Mix 4-6 grams of non-iodized salt with a litre of water and place the salamander in this for up to 72 hours. Ensure that it can raise its head above water level easily. However, it can be very hard to get a salamander to sit in this solution for any length of time.

When preparing a salt solution for treating a salamander, be careful to get the quantities of salt and water right.

- If this does not work, a larger amount of salt (between 10 and 25 grams) can be added to a litre of water. At this high level of salt content, only place the salamander in the solution for a maximum of 20 minutes.
- Types of salt that can be used include sea salt, freshwater aquarium salt and kosher salt. Never use table salt.
- Set up another cage to use while you are treating your salamander. Once you have taken it out of its usual cage, remove everything and clean it thoroughly so that its cage is ready for it when its treatment is complete.

This salamander is being treated for fungal infections. Its body is covered by the treated water while its head is above the water level.

Internal parasites

Any **wild-caught** amphibian is likely to have worms unless a sample of faeces has been taken and shown to be free from **parasites**. Since parasites slow the animal's growth rates and make them more likely to pick up disease, it is sensible to worm mature animals at least once a year. If left untreated, parasites can cause death.

Microscopic nematode worms can infect salamanders and make them sick.

External parasites

Any aquatic salamander can develop external parasites, some of which are the same as those found on fish. It can be very hard to see the difference between these, a bacterial infection and a skin problem.

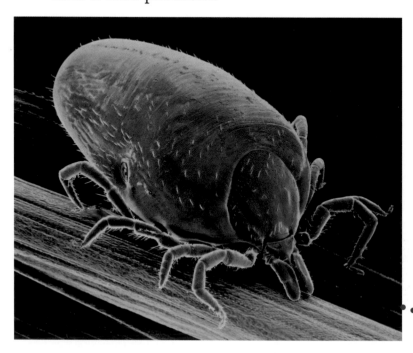

Ticks can infect your salamander and cause poor health. Make sure you inspect your pet's skin regularly for such external parasites.

Abscesses

Any wound that becomes infected can develop into an abscess (an infected area of tissue). Common problems include poor hygiene, overcrowding and any cause of stress. If territorial animals are kept together with insufficient space to form separate territories, one will attack any others and this may cause an abscess to occur. Treatment is by surgical removal of the abscess and making sure that whatever caused it is put right.

Top tip

Remember that if you are in any doubt about what is wrong with your salamander, contact your veterinarian for advice before you start to treat it.

Fluid retention

If you notice that your salamander appears very 'fat' for no obvious reason, such as just after eating a meal, then it may be suffering from fluid retention. In this situation a veterinary surgeon must be contacted as the animal may well need a course of antibiotics to save its life. It is important to try to get your pet to the veterinarian as soon as possible to allow it the best chance of making a recovery.

This salamander looks fatter than it should. It may be suffering from fluid retention.

You must contact your veterinarian immediately if you are concerned about your salamander's health.

When a salamander dies

If, to the best of your ability, you provide your salamander with an ideal enclosure, try hard to recreate its natural **habitat** and give it a good diet, it should live for more than 14 years. Some keepers have claimed it is possible for salamanders to live for up to 50 years!

When your salamander gets old it might become less active and rest a lot.

But no matter what you do for your pet, one day it will inevitably die. Some pet salamanders die peacefully in their sleep, but at other times it may have to be a joint decision taken by you and the veterinarian in order to prevent your pet from suffering unnecessarily. It is never easy to make the decision to let the vet give your salamander an overdose of anaesthetic that will send it off to sleep. Part of you will always want that extra day to take your pet home and say goodbye privately. However, if your salamander is in pain then, as a true friend, you will need to be strong and allow the veterinarian to end any suffering in a quiet and painless manner.

It is always
upsetting when
a much-loved
pet is ill, or dies.

Feeling upset

Whether your pet passes away in its sleep or
at the veterinary surgery, you will feel upset.
It is perfectly normal to cry when you think
of your pet leaving your life. After a period
of time the pain will gradually become less
and then you will remember the happy
times the two of you spent together.

Making a
special burial
place for your
pet can help
you feel better.

Keeping records

To help decide whether or not your pet is doing well, it is important to keep accurate records of its growth and development on your computer or in a notebook. Over a period of time it is very difficult to remember whether your salamander fed or went to the toilet on certain days over the past few weeks, let alone months, so a record book will remind you of important behavioural changes, and daily patterns.

Records help to tell you if you need to see the veterinarian and copies of them should be taken with you if you decide to go to the veterinary clinic. This information will make sure that the veterinarian knows exactly why you are concerned and then help to identify anything that is out of the ordinary.

Photos are a great way of remembering how you first made friends with your pet.

Why not keep photos of your salamander in your record book?

You could add other types of records to your scrapbook too. In your free time you can gather a collection of photographs of the two of you together at different stages in your salamander's life. You can use these to produce a scrapbook charting the different stages in your relationship with your pet.

More fun

Why not have a 'Pet Day' at your home one weekend; simply invite some of your closest friends on the day that your salamander needs cleaning. Ask your friends to write a story about salamanders on a piece of paper, mount this on a piece of brightly coloured card, and decorate your room with the stories and pictures your friends have created. Invite a different friend each week to come over and help you clean your pet. This makes cleaning fun, and shortens the length of time it takes to keep the cage clean.

You could draw pictures of your pet and show them to your friends at school.

Glossary

amphibian   animal that lives both in and out of water

antibacterial   drug which destroys bacteria and so prevents and cures bacterial infections

breeding season   time of year when animals mate to produce young

captive-bred   grown under the control of humans, not in the wild

carnivorous   mainly meat eating

colony   group of creatures that live together

daphnia   tiny water fleas that are related to crabs and shrimps

dehydrate   to dry out or to lose water in the body enough to cause discomfort or illness

draught   a current of cool air in a closed space

fungus   type of living thing that gets food by absorbing other living or decaying material (plural = fungi)

gills   feathery organs used by organisms such as fish, designed to obtain oxygen in water

gland   organ of the body which makes special substances such as hormones or digestive juices

habitat   place where an animal or plants lives or grows

herpetology   the study of reptiles and amphibians

hide   place for animal to take shelter from predators, sunshine or rain

humidity   moisture in the air

infestation   presence (of parasites) in large numbers, often to cause damage or disease

larva   the young form or stage of an animal , which is usually different in shape from the adult, and which spends much time feeding (plural = larvae)

maintain   keep at the same level or rate, keeping in good condition by checking on something regularly

metamorphose   to undergo a series of changes in appearance when changing from immature form into adult form

mite   small creature that lives on another animal's skin and sucks its blood

neuter   to perform an operation that stops salamanders from having babies

nocturnal   active at night

parasite   small creatures, such as ticks and worms, that live on or in another animal's body and usually harm them

porous   describes a material that has tiny spaces through which liquids or gases can pass

predator   hunter, animal that hunts and kills other animals for food

reptile   cold-blooded animal with scaly or rough skin

respiratory   affecting breathing

solitary   alone

species   a kind or particular sort of living creature

sphagnum moss   special kind of moss

stress   mental or emotional strain

substrate   soft material to put in the bottom of the salamander cage

terrarium   cage for amphibians or reptiles

tetanus   a disease caused by bacteria

ultraviolet light   invisible (to humans) part of light that is used to produce vitamin D in salamander's skin

vaccination   an injection that is given to protect against a disease

vivarium   cage for amphibians or reptiles

wild-caught   captured by humans from the wild

Useful addresses

International Herpetological Society
c/o Mrs Carol Friend
15 Barnett Lane
Wordsley
West Midlands DY8 5PZ
United Kingdom
http://www.international-herp-society.co.uk

Exotic Animal Welfare Trust
Boundary Cottage Farm
Inkerman
Towlaw DL13 4QB
United Kingdom
http://www.eawt.org

More books to read

Newts and Salamanders (A Complete Pet Owner's Manual), Frank Indivigilo (Barrons Educational Series, 1997)

Salamanders and Newts as a New Pet, John Coburn (TFH Publications, 1995)

Helpful websites

http://www.exoticpets.about.com/cs/salamanders – Advice on how to care for salamanders.

http://www.enature.com – Go to 'Amphibians' and then select 'Salamanders'. Gives lots of information about different species.

http://www.caudata.org – Good information about salamanders.

http://www.mavicanet.ru/directory/eng/18427.htm – Gives a listing of herpetological societies in the USA.

Index

abscesses   40
amphibians   4, 5, 9, 13, 24, 28, 34, 36, 38

biting   22, 29
breeding season   6, 11, 28, 29
buying your salamander   5, 10, 11

cage furniture   18
captive-bred salamanders   5, 10, 11, 20

death   14, 15, 25, 33, 35, 39, 42–3
dehydration   4, 9
disease carriers   9, 12, 36
draughts   13, 14

faeces   25, 39
female salamanders   11
fighting   11, 40
fire salamanders   6, 7, 9, 11, 13, 14, 28, 29, 31
fluid retention   41
food and water   5, 8, 9, 12, 19, 20–3
fungal infections   25, 38–9

glands   4

handling your salamander   9, 26, 27, 29, 33, 36
health   15, 25, 34–41
herpetological societies   5, 11, 16, 18, 24
hides   18, 32
holiday care   24
humidity   12, 14, 15, 25
hygiene   19, 27, 29, 36, 40

insect food   9, 10, 12, 21, 22, 23

keeping more than one salamander   11, 28, 29, 40

larvae (baby salamanders)   4, 20, 21
lifespan   7, 9, 42

male salamanders   11, 29
mealworms and wax worms   20, 21, 23
metamorphosis   4, 21
misting   15

nail care   24
neutering   34
nocturnal habits   7, 12

parasites   12, 35, 39–40
pets, other   12, 28, 29
plants   18
pluses and minuses of salamanders   8–9, 31, 33
poison   4, 18
predators   4, 18, 31

record book   44–5
reptiles   4
respiratory problems   15

Salmonella   36
size and weight   6, 28
skin   4, 9, 10, 14, 16, 38
skin infections   15, 38-9
skin, shedding   5, 15
species of salamander   6
stress   26, 27, 33, 40
substrate   17, 32

temperature   5, 12, 14, 35
terrarium   9, 11, 12–14, 16-19, 26, 27, 28, 29, 32
terrarium cleaning   17, 19, 36, 37, 45
tiger salamanders   6, 7, 9, 11, 13, 14, 21, 28, 29, 31
transporting your salamander   25
travelling box   25

ultraviolet light   16

vaccinations   34
ventilation   13, 14, 25
veterinarian treatment   9, 25, 34–5, 41, 42, 44
vitamin and mineral supplements   23
wild salamanders   4, 5, 6, 10, 13, 20, 35, 38
worming   35, 39

zoonoses   9, 36

Titles in the *Keeping Unusual Pets* series include:

Hardback   0 431 12414 0

Hardback   0 431 12415 9

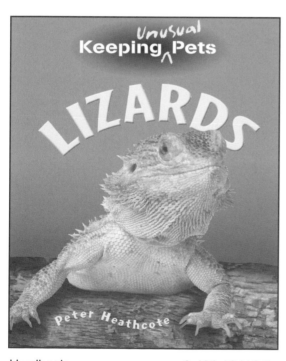

Hardback   0 431 12416 7

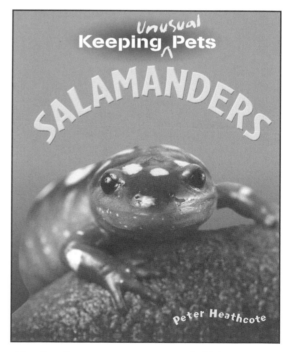

Hardback   0 431 12417 5

Find out about the other titles in this series on our website www.heinemann.co.uk/library